Moments

Out Of

Time

Ina Whitlock

Also by the Author:

Eating the Chinese Pear
travelogue-memoir

Of Love and Loss
poetry

Sketches from Paraguaná
Venezuela, half a century ago

Stories of a Midwest Childhood
1930s–'40s

Origins • Endings
poetry

Published in the United States by
Spirit Journey Books, Vashon Island, Washington
iwhitlock@centurytel.net
www.InaWhitlock.com

Design by Novak Creative, Inc.
Author photo by Jenn Reidel

ISBN-13: 978-0-9859929-2-7

Printed in the United States of America

DEDICATION

I dedicate this book to my extended family,
children, grandchildren, and great-grandchildren,
in the hope of bringing my concerns for the future
into words, and to express my faith that poetry
is one way to bring enlightened consciousness
to man and womankind.

ACKNOWLEDGEMENTS

I am indebted to the Vashon Poets Laureate group
of poets and lovers of poetry for their blessing and
inspiration. To all those who have given their generous
encouragement, my sincere appreciation.

My special thanks to poets Hunter Davis and
Eric Horsting for reading the manuscript
and offering valuable suggestions. Without the editing
and technical assistance of Nancy Morgan,
Eagle Eye Proofreading & Editing,
this book would not be in print.

CONTENTS

Life flowering—
drawn from shadow
to sunlight in a Mason jar
—Dahlias
at the breakfast table.

Word On A Page

This word, my forever now,
  here on the page, I form it.

How was I to know
  when the word was not there,
  a moment of grounding—
  before I'd fallen?—that not

The artfully sculpted shell
  or bone distilled marrow,
  but in unfolding atoms
  is life's longing for life.

Defined by spectrum's light,
  a plethora of days holds
  no form of past or possibility
  on ennui's dark edge.

The lost becomes word,
  the forever now, here
  on the page, I form it,
  enfold it, by this I am.

Instructions To The Artist

If the artist finds vagary of color
recording the breeze
on the grist of an ordinary day,
let painterly hands guide sight
in a magnifying lens,
a singular, silvery weed,
or perhaps a budding flower,
nourished by the brush of acrylic
or watercolor washing a page
with meaning beyond tints
or shades of drifting vapors,
catching movement of pen on paper,
devising the artist's portrait
of what remains.

SYLVAN TAPESTRY

In deep ravines of ancient hills
   weavings of fern, lichen, fir boughs
   become in sun's golden aperture,
   a verdancy, a filigree midday,
   a paisley shawl of leaves and vines
   entwined in nature's artful stitchery,
   'til evening's shadows dull
   to night's deep anonymity.

THE PRESENT HAUNTING

In fleeting gists of moments lived,
   past occasionally returns
   to form the present, as if time
   had not intervened or taken
   whatever measurement of hurt
   or love from the *now* of yesterdays,
   pulling a quilt of years
   over a body's cuts and tears,
   unraveled patterns directed
   or randomly stitched together.

Cascade Of The Spirits

Sadness, a silver thread
   entwines the unknown path I walk
      unsure in mind's grey fog.
Sudden sharp splitting of bones,
   ancient Araucaria tree, thunderous,
      falls into a swirling pool,
   dead leaves still quivering, and I also.

Chile

GRACE

Triangle of white tail
  under-feathers pale,
  black-winged bellows
  —great Bald Eagle—
  raptor, lands in spring hay
  so close, I flutter
  watching the watcher's
  crescent beak, gold eye
  scanning rodent prey.

I want the moment to stay,
  but in rapid flapping
  —Bald Eagle gone—
  I am left to count
  the blessing of
  this uncommon day.

Easter Sunday, 2015

TRILLIUM

Trinity of the three-petaled
   floral blessing of mountain glades,
rhizome spirit, ethereal, perennial,
   fragile, flowering precursor of
summer's sway, under the sacred cedar,
   where I kneel to its subtleties,
a gentleness in complexity, and yet

Other three-mantled elements
   —tritium, strontium, plutonium—
leak from containment toward
   the mother river, Columbia,
where particles blow east, flow west,
     a trinity of elements
     degrading in ecocide
     for an eternity, and yet

I pray the three-petaled Trillium
   blossoms for the next millennium.

WHY

Why paradisical sheaves of summer
    in artful plentitude shower
    this moment in the soft caress
    of peace—when elsewhere,
    war shadows fall and flames devour,
    searing earth and sky, striking
    lives in famine or deluge, while I
    seek for any sign of surety,
    unable to forget the pain-raking
    discrepancy of this sun-filled hour.

THE TURNING

Entranced by the hum
   of an otherworldly scheme
   where clouds break bread
   and wine of darkness
   at dawn is offered in prayer
   —I turn not away, but to the Other.

KAUAI MORNING CALLS

Wonder of a waking world,
  first wild chick's cluck
  a peep, a pecking song—
  the furtive *wheyly bup, bup, bup.*

Cackles and trills spill
  into sky's awakening,
  sounds of *witsi, witsi, witsi,*
  and *to weet, to weet   yu roo.*

Bird arias, dozens,
  sweeter than human song
  forth and back in dialogue
  'til midday mountain flight.

A musical return, reprieve
  late afternoon, of *tee vit, tee vit,*
  yu roo   and *witsi, witsi, witsi,*
  bringing evening in.

With a *die, die sis*, a *purty, purty chu,*
  and night's last fading *furdia, furdia,*
  'til morning calls again—
  with a *wheyly bup, bup, bup!*

World, wake up! up! up!

WINGED FLIGHT

Flight on wings—fragile,
  as all things seem,
yet toughness of thin bones
—the feathered ones—
swift in strong dance
  weaving earth to air,
while trails of gossamer
  disperse in CO_2
the whine and drone
  of metallic birds,
shredding time and meridians
  with no birdsong—
    and yet, I long to fly.

WHERE WE ARE

Summer daze, Puccini and Butterfly,
  lethargy that drains all thought,
  melancholy ennui
  floating on listless air,
  watery vision that a ship
  on the horizon would save all
  from betrayal, ambition, politics,
  that brought us here
  to face the coming heat.

inspired by Giacomo Puccini's opera,
Madama Butterfly
    Butterfly's betrayal by Pinkerton

THIS AIR WE BREATHE *Fukushima 2012*

Air, gentle, warming the skin,
   a benevolence we breathe effortlessly

Treasured conduit of light, sunlight
   of a living planet beguiled by beauty

Fair days, deceived by winds of change,
   appearance counts for nothing

But buttons do, that Sendai children wear
   weighing curies of radiation

Invisible, mutagenic, menace of particles
   strontium, cesium, plutonium.

Pluto, biting dog at our heels,
   melted core, fuel rods, monitors

Measured in half-lives, that cannot slow
   isotopes working in thyroid and bone.

END GAME

An angry sun wakened day,
  blotting stains on heaven
  in particulates of CO_2,
  edges of Earth's garments
  stitched in fragile threads,
  profusion of seeds and grasses
  lashed by winds, seas lapping
  at limbs of sustainability,
  and our loss of ability to gauge
  the thrust, or comprehend
  geologic annals of history
  in rock, shift, rift, scree,
  the slow, now quickening
  impoverishment in entropy,
  breathless void, foul air,
  rare domain where science
  is useless as a compass
  unless compassionate intent
  overtakes the spell.

OVERHEAD

Earth's strident rhythms
   lost in peacefulness above—
up here, grounding is a mountain's ridge,
   a flow of arabesque and cuneiform
streaming subliminal messages
   in riverbeds, unmapped particulars,
forests, farmlands squared, where life
   contains the known, curved byways
of intention leading through clouds of doubt,
   at city's edge a centrifugal force,
intensity and density in mass
   stretching seams of consciousness
beyond the hum of happenstance
   —evolving in our sense of being
      on Earth in peace.

QUESTION

I asked, and then made answer
as best I could, knowing only
moments lived, not written on a page
but in a flow of feelings on the clasp,
the rasp of pain, or shock of catastrophe,
or in the best of days when perception
colors layers of remembrance,
or makes possible a grasp of life
beyond faith or images, unencumbered,
somewhere beyond the watch of time
—then may I know answer
to the question posed
—where does the soul survive?

INTERPRETATION

When civilizations require less time
to be destroyed than rise—Hiroshima,
Aleppo; a continuum of evidence:
Jerash, Mycenae, Ozymandias,
ruins in sands of history—visions
lost, alchemy of spirit opened
on papyrus, clay tablets, mind's ontological
studies, a legacy of words and clues,
illusions, acquisitions, greed,
inquisitors, spoilers of the hour
thrusting flags in starts and failings,
circuitry routed in fractious minds,
lacking what is required when ground
quakes on sands of forgetfulness, yet,
new paths of invention counter with
possibilities of gain from loss—
    patterns that in a dying leaf, might bring
    new meaning and interpretation.

"Look At Me," She Said

I noticed first the upheld cup,
then a smashed, dark face looking up
from the city's sidewalk, and I heard her say
in a fervent, grating way, "Please, help me!"

Others passing ignored her, as I did,
though I made attempt to reason why
or why not give her change from my pocket,
thinking the hopelessness of such endeavor
—that nothing could take her (or others)
from such degradation—hers a life
on the street, mine in comfort
of health and home.

Crossing with a green light,
nothing to stop me from going on,
I tried to forget that crabbed self, holding a cup
to passersby who did not look at her,
even when she placed a frayed jacket sleeve
on the walkway, to trap them, I supposed.

And I waited on the corner across the street,
watching to see if any coins would fall
in her cup, wondering if for food or drugs
she held out her hand, or for some madness
without discernment of just how things were?

And I watched, hidden by jutting concrete,
then shifted to a newspaper stand
and a city light pole where I kept post,
watching until a not so well dressed gentleman
dropped something in her cup,
then a woman, perhaps reluctantly,
gave change from her purse.

I wondered if she saw me loitering
in my orange jacket, or if her eyes
even had sight enough, but something changed
in my boarded-up heart and I walked back
when the streetlight said 'Go.'

"You remind me," I said, "of someone dear,"
which wasn't a lie, but the truth of a friend,
and when I said it again, she understood,
and abruptly stood up, saying, "Give me a hug!"
And I did, taking my eye-shades off to look
in her eyes, and put but a dollar in her cup.

"Look at me," she pleaded,
pointing to her shoe (someone's old Ked),
toes showing through the sole's whole side,
and before I could think, she hobbled off,
her howl splitting heaven into a hell
that sears city streets.

Uncommon To The Eye

Cement walkway, dusty, dull,
  walked on, walked over
  by everyone and me, until
  in a slant of sun nearing the horizon,
  the rude, grey cement dissolves,
  sparkling like stars in a darkening
  Cosmos where, at twilight hour,
  I see what I've overlooked before.

WALKING THIN AIR

Trapped in private worlds, insular
travelers, feet bound, walking thin air
in darkness not of their making;
the guy with mud on hiking boots,
blond in pink sandals, carefully
peeling a banana, while young ones
sleep on the floor, transported
from a cavernous airport in dreams,
stuffed lion under curly heads.

Where do they come from, where
do they go, those dozing in rows
waiting at a gate for lives to begin?

A boy and his sister play cards,
lively, awake, speaking Spanish
in clever parlance lost to me
for lack of caffeine, or tea leaves
to read the situation I'm in.

Others, deep in waves of sleep,
flights canceled, are like birds
waiting morning light as the languor
of night takes hold, while I wish
for dawn that never comes, when
all I wanted was a connection in Detroit.

Where have they gone, the beautiful
blond in pink sandals, the guy
in mud-boots, worldly-wise facades,
travelers shuttered like the coffee stands
with nothing to share until morning.

PAST RETURNED

Unexpected flight back in time—
  reprise—
  music in an airport women's room
  transporting me to Latin otherness,
  rhythm of Joropo and harp,
  flurry of heart strings
  in each swirl of skirt as we danced,
  reinventing ourselves

  —but, I am here, another self—
  waiting for a flight to Albuquerque.

musica Llanera
Venezuela

MUSE MUSEUM

Artifacts not held in hand, or seen,
structured from cells' memory,
synapses fired, signs perceived
in mind's Muse Museum.

Dream visuals transformed
in deep space mystery,
a sleepless sun circling history,
planet awash in liquidity,

Tapestry of rivers in brain's neurology,
ghost harvesters of civilizations
lifting stones, domes, stelas, spires,
in ancient fields of temporality.

NEW MOON

New moon suddenly unearthed
From our dark side,
Orb rising full observed.

Mark of phases in our lives,
Muse of passions and content,
Mother/father of our history,
Keeper of our tides and time,
Sage of faceless imagery
We stood before and stared
Through ageless mists of mind,
'Til that July when millions
Crossed the uncommitted void
To score that virgin silt as ours,
Dispel romantic mystery,
Reduce the magnitude of shine
With rocks in chemical analysis
And realms of other moons beyond.

Apollo 11
1969

THE AGENTS

Neural pathways of possibility,
   mitochondrial cells, conduits
   of a body's universe,
   particulates we breathe,
   degrees of telluric energies,
   bombarding milliseconds
   traced in cyber games we play,
   icons, ipads, agents of plasticity,
   cityscapes and nationalities,
   referential guides, our numbers
   analogued and digitized.

Theorem

If living only in abstraction
of Schrodinger's theory
of the boxed cat in two places
dead or alive at once, unless
observed, one way or the other

Are we holding space only
in mind, where dreams and duty
rule; a Yin and Yang
of amplitude in characters
devising changing roles?

Are we a multitude of virtual
or real, as in Bell's theory of
non-locality, milliseconds
of energy constantly blinking
out and in, two places at once,

Particles of an undecipherable
universe of souls seeking self,
manifesting in alpha/delta waves
of the Here and There,
of Now and Then,

Alive in non-locality, unless, or when
Schrodinger's cat escapes the trap?

Full Moon

Clouds chasing the moon—
visceral wisps on my body
assailed in night's drifting vigil,
jagged rock scenarios,
shipwrecked catastrophes
—no strobe of reason,
no light of day.

FIREFLIES

Have fireflies lost their reason for being
or are they lost
because we do not remember them?

Out there, on summer evenings
beyond city lights, do they still dance
or only in nights of childhood?

Sudden magical displays,
glowing off and on, fervently sought
as we run barefoot in the grass.

Fanciful phenomena,
if caught in a lidded jar,
wandering beacons, gone by day.

Lightning bugs
detached from wings, wonderment
of magical ring-finger displays.

Luciferin glow of cells, attracting
a male or prey, Lucifer lighting up
in gardens of our youth.

Darkness, vital necessity to survive,
lost in lights of halogen,
dimming prospects of ever being seen.

FOLLOWING FLIGHT

Flight into the future—
  the eternal now,
   velocity of spirit flowing
    in quantum particles and waves,
     complicity of galaxies, star seeds,
      random nano-sparks
       in gravity of time—when
       one small wail of history
      arrives from cells' invention,
    child surviving the thrust of life
   in the ethereal interval
  between the blink and flash
of the I Am, we are.

GLOBAL CHANGE

How is it possible to discover
a star 600 million light years beyond Earth
that might sustain life, when here
we are unable to sustain civility
and killing is the real and unreal game?

The notion that thought is not reality—
that what we do,
or what we believe,
does not carry poison or perfume
into our lives and the lives of others.

What is required to understand
the dark nature of our being
as we invade the moon and Mars,
when technical inventions change
more rapidly than laws give equanimity?

Superseding capacity to know,
without necessity to comprehend, we are
unable to believe the warnings or connect
money, politics, and global change to
suffering, loss, unless we are the victims.

IMPERMANENCE

By whatever configuration
   or entity, or seeming space,
   whatever vision, or conundrum
   of near possibility—
   I had no intention of confronting this:

Living the good life, otherwise occupied
   when industrial winter came,
   high temperatures and rising seas
   following calibrated lines,
   I read time's message well.

Detonations, exodus, and nuclear debris,
   virtual dark matter and closed minds,
   toxic air, neuro-toxic pesticides,
   failed crops and water lack
   —God and Nature not responsible—

only *we* are capable, if we have time.

SHORE

Walk this shore of transient waves
  escaping to sunlight's enfoldment
  of stones, concretions, shells,
  accidental patterning in sands
  reversing, turning again, so small
  an incident of planetary time.

BLANKET OF BREEZE

Five swim-clad girls sprawl
   prone, turning shrimp-pink,
   uropod feet swimming sky,
   cloud puffs above, waves
   quickening a blanket of breeze.

uropod: the tailfan of shrimp

Sea Song

Rim of waves flowing
   fathoms deep to undertow,
   grist of sand underfoot,
   spume drift glistening,
   shells chattering on shallows,
   lapping tongues of the ancestors
   singing tides in and out
   on bottles of rum and ale
   with rhyme of ballad and song

   'til gull's sudden cry—
   breakers breaking,
   hearts breaking down
   on chimeras of cosmic ides.

MARY CASSATT'S
"CHILDREN PLAYING ON THE BEACH"
—1884

Just outside the frame, sister,
   dig your shovel deep
   in sands of time
   where I wished for you,
   sister (or brother) I never had,
   to be here with us,
   the sisters I now embrace
   as we play on the shores of our days,
   cherishing each other.

READER IN THE LIBRARY

Seated, heavy set, old black cap on bent head,
glasses low, a man of middle age.

Are you waiting, or perusing the library's
magazine for an evening in from the cold,
fingering pages, stopping at an article
on Africa, drawn to children standing
in a desolate room, legs torn from bodies,
propped on crutches—the lucky ones.

Reader, browsing, you travel to Africa
for a moment, perhaps touching some sorrow,
or tasting bitterness of life, theirs and your own,
cradling the magazine on upturned knees,
scruffy shoes, dirt encrusted, as if you've been
foot slogging in your own Africa.

Curious when I get up, I see the strange scissors
attached to your coat, strung from your neck
as if you might cut bad scenes from this world
and your life.

Sound Of Green

In the beginning, crisp leaves underfoot,
    cells disintegrating, channels of discord,
    weather awry, drought, deluge, fire,
    no one cause, but all signals of shift,
    warnings beyond ability to heal, unless
    clearing distractions and neglect,
    in quietude—we hear
    green whispering the trees.

CAMELLIAS

One instant, one shift, or accident of truth
   changes a lifetime—a swift vision,
   no moment to deflect the incident—
   the arrow does not bend the shaft, but
   cuts before—from after—out of time.

Camellias, there at the window
   —suddenly gone—cut to a stub,
   mind unable to comprehend
   the lack, the visceral surety of green,
   a greeting as it should have been.

No tenderness of pink blossoms
   as I hurry to the phone
   —see nothing—Camellias gone,
   hear the unexpected
   voice of death and vacancy.

I Am, You Are

When boundaries fall on dusk's gold rim,
   then no adversity or distance mars
     dark death, but light encodes
in conscious word, a language
     without form, unmeasured, unspoken,
the You and I—made singular
    in love's complicity, and that
      is all I need to know.

SHIMMER

Shimmer,
   as if you might disappear
   in a stream of dappling brightness
   or shadow, a melody, a Scheherazade
   of themes, gentle shifts, a youthful
   breathing in and singing out,
   as if the whole of life lives in sway
   of self's inner resounding stream,
   a drift of minor themes, or major dreams,
   river's dark dazzling eddies not easily
   convened in calm, lost in musical notes,
   a conversation of cellos, flutes, violins
   that transcends meaning
   in sorrow and escape,
   with nothing to capture, nothing to save
   but the silent, tender nuances
   —of an ode to moments lived.

Scheherazade: symphonic poem
composed by Rimsky-Korsakov, 1888

NAMELESS ATTRIBUTE

In the name of God, the gods, or All That Is,
   the wonders of the universe,
   each human birth, each birth of animal,
   each plant, each drop of water,
   cloud or gathering storm,
   the plight of the homeless, wounded,
   cry of hunger beyond hearing,
   where we the well-living dwell
   walled in entropy of plentitude
   —unless we look deeply in the many
   colored lens of humankind and see
   in a child's stare an old soul of eternity
   —then can we know Divinity.

LAST

Slow disintegration cell by cell,
   absence of acuity,
   light waves unraveling,
   no bell of warning,
   only flutter of particle and wave,
   dusting of cosmic pulse
   filtering sound with language,
   first rending cry, to last whimper,
   desire sustained by inner fire,
   a planetary glow on neurons'
   galactic, uncharted fields.

Horizon of sea waves far tumbling
near wavelets sluicing paths
to insight and healing,
on shores of consciousness
a single grain of sand.

Poet Laureate
of Vashon Island, Washington 2013–2015,
Ina Whitlock continues to write poetry and prose,
and to create art.